The Legend of
Dracula

Gareth Stevens
PUBLISHING

By
Michael Sabatino

Please visit our website, www.garethstevens.com. For a free color catalog of all our high-quality books, call toll free 1-800-542-2595 or fax 1-877-542-2596.

Library of Congress Cataloging-in-Publication Data

Sabatino, Michael.
The legend of Dracula / by Michael Sabatino.
p. cm. — (Famous legends)
Includes index.
ISBN 978-1-4824-2732-5 (pbk.)
ISBN 978-1-4824-2733-2 (6 pack)
ISBN 978-1-4824-2734-9 (library binding)
1. Stoker, Bram, — 1847-1912. — Dracula — Juvenile literature. 2. Dracula, Count (Fictitious character) —Juvenile literature. 3. Vlad — III, — Prince of Wallachia, — 1430 or 1431-1476 or 1477 — Juvenile literature. I. Sabatino, Michael. II. Title.
PR6037.T617 S23 2016
823'.8—d23

First Edition

Published in 2016 by
Gareth Stevens Publishing
111 East 14th Street, Suite 349
New York, NY 10003

Designer: Laura Bowen
Editor: Therese Shea

Photo credits: Cover, p. 1 (Dracula) CSA Images/Mod Art Collection/Vetta/Getty Images; cover, p. 1 (night sky) Stanislav Pobytov/Vetta/Getty Images; cover, p. 1 (ribbon) barbaliss/Shutterstock.com; cover, p. 1 (leather) Pink Pueblo/Shutterstock.com; cover, pp. 1–32 (sign) Sarawut Padungkwan/Shutterstock.com; cover, pp. 1–32 (vines) vitasunny/Shutterstock.com; cover, pp. 1–32 (parchment) TyBy/Shutterstock.com; cover, pp. 1–32 (background) HorenkO/Shutterstock.com; p. 4 CSA Images/Printstock Collection/Vetta/Getty Images; p. 5 Marco Cristofori/Robert Harding World Imagery/Getty Images; pp. 7 (main), 10, 11 Hulton Archive/Stringer/Getty Images; p. 7 (inset) Carl Savich/Wikimedia Commons; p. 9 Silver Screen Collection/Moviepix/Getty Images; p. 13 (main) Amandajm/Wikimedia Commons; p. 13 (inset) Universal Pictures/Handout/Moviepix/Getty Images; p. 15 (main) John Kobal Foundation/Moviepix/Wikimedia Commons; p. 15 (inset) Cekli829/Wikimedia Commons; p. 17 (map) Andrein/Wikimedia Commons; p. 17 (garlic) JJ Harrison/Wikimedia Commons; p. 19 Imagno/Hulton Archive/Getty Images; p. 21 Universal Images Group/Wikimedia Commons; p. 23 (main) John William Waterhouse/Wikimedia Commons; p. 23 (inset) John William Polidori/Wikimedia Commons; p. 25 (main) Archive Photos/Stringer/Moviepix/Getty Images; p. 25 (inset) Universal/Wikimedia Commons; p. 27 Regis Martin/Getty Images; p. 29 © iStockphoto.com/PictureLake.

Printed in the United States of America

CPSIA compliance information: Batch #CS15GS: For further information contact Gareth Stevens, New York, New York at 1-800-542-2595.

Contents

Lurking in a Castle 4

The Legend Is Born 6

A Taste for Blood 8

A Scary Ship 10

A Reign of Terror 12

A Fight Against Time 14

Borrowing Lore 16

Take a Stab at It 18

The Real Dracula 20

A Bloody History 22

Rise to Fame 24

Vampires Among Us 26

Dracula Lives On 28

Glossary 30

For More Information 31

Index 32

Words in the glossary appear in **bold** type the first time they are used in the text.

Lurking in a Castle

As the sun sinks, daylight slips into darkness. Somewhere deep within an unwelcoming castle, something dangerous stirs. A monster rises from his **coffin**, his sharp teeth glowing in the moonlight. It's Dracula! He has awoken, and he's thirsty for blood.

Chances are, you've heard of Dracula, the world-famous vampire. Many movies have been made about him. But where did such a scary **legend** come from? As you'll discover, Dracula is based on a real and terrifying person!

Many call Bran Castle in Transylvania "Dracula's Castle."

The Legend Is Born

In 1897, the book *Dracula* by Bram Stoker was first published. This work introduced the world to the fearsome character Count Dracula. It wasn't a best seller at first, but it became very popular.

In Stoker's story, Dracula lived in an old castle in Transylvania, an area located inside the country of Romania. Dracula seemed like a normal nobleman at first. But he kept a dark secret—he was really a vampire who was hundreds of years old!

The Inside Story

The name "Dracula" comes from *dracul* which means "dragon" in Romanian.

Bram Stoker worked for the famed Lyceum Theatre in London, England. He may have based his Dracula character on his friend, actor Henry Irving.

DRACULA

BRAM·STOKER

A Taste for Blood

A vampire is a **mythical** creature with special powers. In Stoker's book, Dracula had superhuman strength and could climb walls like a lizard. Sometimes he would change himself into different animals, such as a bat or a dog. He could even vanish and then reappear somewhere else.

But being a vampire isn't all fun and games. To stay alive, vampires must drink the blood of other people. That's where their **fangs** come in handy!

The Inside Story

Bram Stoker also used the word "nosferatu" for vampires. He probably thought the term meant "undead" in Romanian, though its real meaning is unclear.

Vampires are famous for biting the neck of their **victims** to drink their blood.

9

A Scary Ship

In Stoker's story, Dracula left his native land for England in search of fresh blood. But being a vampire was a hard secret to keep. On the boat ride there, Dracula had to feed on the blood of crew members to survive. One by one, they mysteriously disappeared from the ship until only the captain was left.

After a terrible storm, the boat ran aground. Witnesses saw a large dog jump from the ship. It was really Dracula making his escape to England!

Artwork featured vampires long before Stoker's book.

11

A Reign of Terror

Dracula terrorized London, seeking out new victims at night and feasting on their blood. Fresh blood had a strange effect on Dracula. It allowed him to look and feel much younger than his real age.

One of his victims was Lucy Westenra. Her doctor, John Seward, couldn't figure out why she was losing so much blood. Lucy caught the attention of a professor named Abraham Van Helsing. After studying vampire **lore**, Van Helsing recognized the bite marks on the victim's neck as the work of a vampire.

The Inside Story

Lucy later died, but rose again—as a vampire!

Dracula **Historic Personal** Dracula

Doctor of mad house ~~Seward~~ Seward

Girl engaged to him Lucy Westenra school...

Mad Patient { theory of getting life – instinctively go... up idea with mad cunning.

Lawer ~~Arthur~~ ~~Abbott~~ ~~I Luc~~ Peter Hawkins

His clerk ———— Jonathan Harker

Fiancée of above ~~Kate~~ Wilhelmina M...

~~Lawyer~~ ~~Murray~~

~~Historian~~

~~Authoress~~ ———— Kat...

Friend of ~~Schoolfellow~~ of above ————

The Count ————————— Count ~~Wampyr~~

A ~~Deaf~~ Mute woman } English Servants of

A Silent Man } the Count

A Detective ———————————— Cot...

A Psychical Research Agents ————

~~An American Inventor~~ ~~from Texas~~

A German Professor ———— Max Windshoeffel

A Painter ———— Francis M. Aytown

A Texan ———— Brutus M. Marix

These are notes Stoker made about some of the characters in his book.

A Fight Against Time

Van Helsing now knew what he was up against—a dangerously powerful vampire! He formed a small group of vampire hunters, including Lucy's **fiancé** Arthur, her friend Mina, Mina's husband Jonathan, Dr. Seward, and an American cowboy named Quincey Morris. Together, they chased Dracula back to Transylvania.

There, Van Helsing and his group acted quickly. As the sun was about to set, Dracula was cornered. His head was cut off, and a knife was driven into his heart. He turned to dust!

The practice of putting a stake, or wooden post, through the vampire's heart was thought to kill it and pin it to the ground, so it would never rise again from its grave.

Borrowing Lore

Bram Stoker's *Dracula* is possibly the most famous vampire legend of all time. But how did he create such a character? He spent years studying eastern European history and folklore. Stoker borrowed certain practices he learned about for his book, such as using garlic for protection against vampires.

In many ways, Transylvania was the perfect setting for Dracula's home. That part of Europe was known for its vampire lore long before *Dracula* was written. The people there called vampires *strigoi* (stree-GOY).

The Inside Story

Garlic was thought to have many special healing powers, a belief that dates back to ancient Egypt.

"Transylvania" means "across the woods" in Latin.

Transylvania

ROMANIA

Take a Stab at It

Stoker's vampire hunters drove a stake through Dracula's heart to kill him, a method Stoker borrowed from folklore. In fact, this vampire myth was so believable that some dug-up graves have revealed staked bodies!

People think Stoker also found **inspiration** for Dracula in a real-life nobleman from the 1400s known to have a taste for blood: Vlad the **Impaler**. Vlad got his scary nickname because of the terrible way he killed his enemies.

The Inside Story

In the 1700s, fear of vampires gripped parts of eastern Europe. Graves were dug up and bodies of loved ones thought to be vampires were staked and reburied.

Vlad the Impaler fought to rule Walachia, an area in Transylvania.

19

The Real Dracula

Vlad the Impaler's real name might sound familiar to you: Vlad Dracula! He was the son of Vlad Dracul, who ruled Walachia. Following his father's death, Vlad Dracula had to fight the **Ottoman** Empire for control of Walachia.

After winning a battle, Vlad Dracula would often have enemies' bodies impaled on sharp stakes that were set in the ground like flagpoles. Their hanging bodies served as a warning to all: Don't mess with Vlad the Impaler!

The Inside Story

In one account, attacking enemy soldiers turned back after coming upon a forest of impaled bodies Vlad Dracula had left behind.

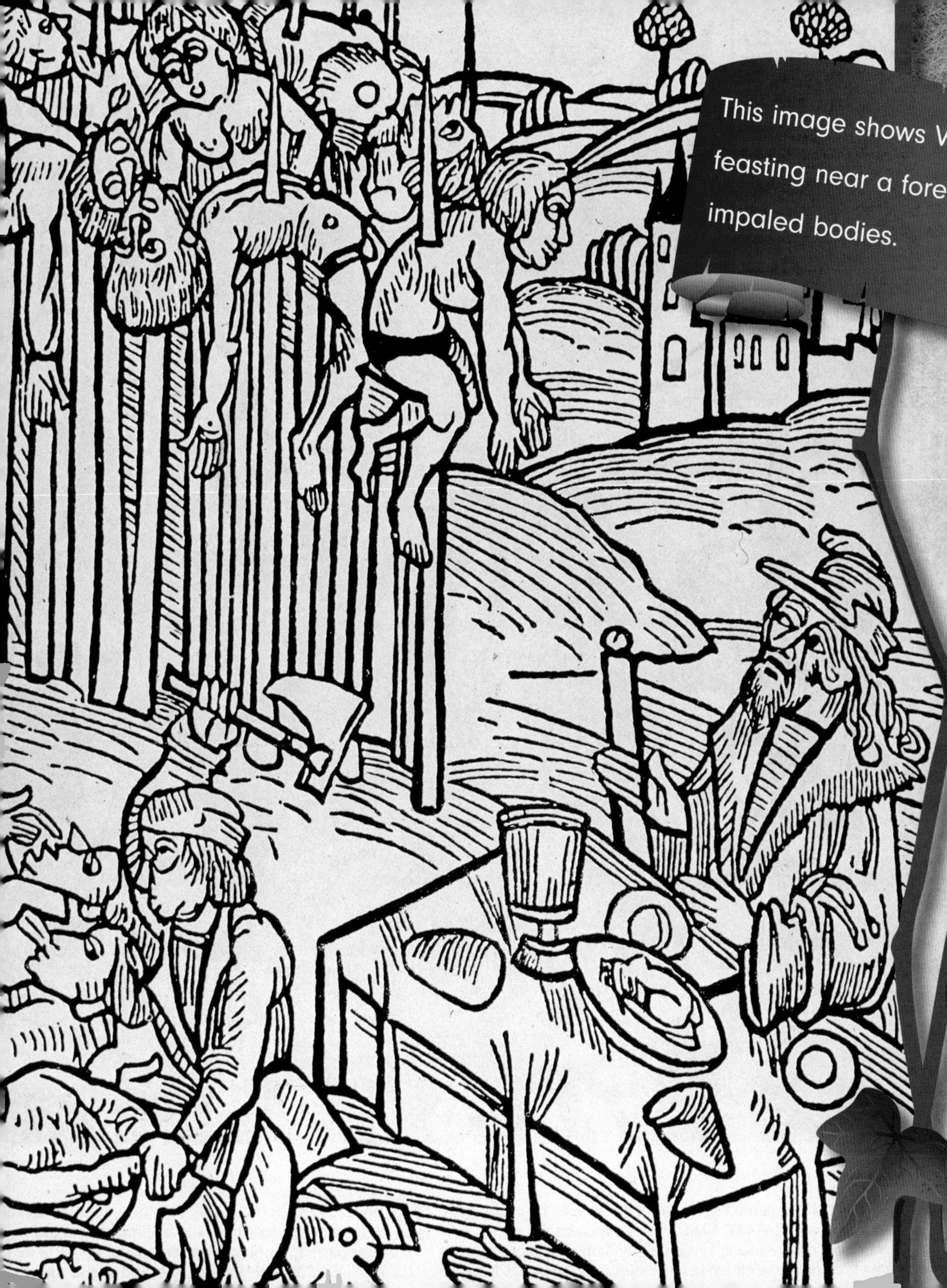

This image shows Vlad Dracula feasting near a forest of impaled bodies.

A Bloody History

Though Dracula is the most famous vampire today, he wasn't the first to appear in a story. The short story "The Vampyre" by John Polidori was published 78 years before *Dracula*. It featured a vampire nobleman named Lord Ruthven.

But long before any book was written about vampires, many ancient **cultures** had evil, bloodthirsty figures in their folklore. According to Greek mythology, the beautiful queen Lamia made Zeus's wife Hera jealous and was doomed by her to feast on blood.

The Inside Story

The ideas for both "The Vampyre" and Frankenstein came about when a group of authors, including Mary Shelley and Lord Byron, got together and told scary stories to one another in 1816.

In this painting, Lamia draws a soldier to her. Her beautiful appearance helped her attract and later eat innocent people!

THE

VAMPYRE;

A Tale.

LONDON:

PRINTED FOR SHERWOOD, NEELY, AND JONES,
PATERNOSTER-ROW.

1819.

[Entered at Stationers' Hall, March 27, 1819.]

23

Rise to Fame

The Dracula we know today became famous thanks to movies. More than 150 movies based in some way on Bram Stoker's book have been made through the years.

However, most consider actor Bela Lugosi's Count Dracula in the 1931 movie *Dracula* to be the most respected. Lugosi gave Dracula a powerful presence on the big screen that was a hit with moviegoers. In fact, most Halloween vampire **costumes** today look like the costume of Lugosi's Dracula.

The Inside Story

Recently, the chupacabra, a bloodsucking animal, has entered modern folklore in parts of the Americas.

After he died, Bela Lugosi was buried wearing his Dracula cape!

Vampires Among Us

You don't have to look very far to see that the legend of Dracula is still going strong today. Comic books, cartoons, video games, and even a breakfast cereal are based on the famous count from Transylvania. And what would Halloween be without trick-or-treaters walking the streets dressed as Dracula? Dracula has made sure the vampire myth remains alive.

Other vampires have entered our culture, too. Books and movies like the *Twilight* series have made vampires more popular than ever.

The Inside Story

The *Twilight* movies have earned over $3 billion worldwide!

Even the Count from *Sesame Street* is based on Dracula. However, he's not meant to be scary.

27

Dracula Lives On

Dracula has left a lasting mark across Europe as well. Visitors travel to Romania to see the mysterious land Dracula called home. **Festivals** are held in Ireland and England to celebrate Stoker and his famous story, too.

Dracula's popularity shows no signs of fading. In the book, Dracula would have lived forever if he hadn't been stopped by the heroes. But it seems that he will continue to live on forever in popular culture!

The Inside Story

In 2000, the Library of Congress added the 1931 movie Dracula to the National Film Registry.

32 USA

Bela Lugosi as

DRACULA

1997

The US Postal Service honored Bela Lugosi and the *Dracula* movie in a stamp in 1997.

Glossary

coffin: a box in which a dead person is buried

costume: clothes that are worn by someone who is trying to look like a different person or thing

culture: the beliefs and ways of life of a group of people

fang: a long, pointed tooth

festival: a special time or event when people gather to celebrate something

fiancé: a man to whom a woman is engaged to be married

impaler: one who causes a pointed object to go into or through something or someone

inspiration: something that makes someone want to do something or that gives someone an idea about what to do or create

legend: a story that has been passed down for many, many years that's unlikely to be true

lore: traditional knowledge or belief

mythical: like a legend or story

Ottoman: relating to the Turkish Empire begun in the late 13th century in western Asia. It ended in 1922.

victim: someone who is hurt or killed by someone or something

For More Information

Books

Ganeri, Anita, and David West. *Outlaws and Villains from History.* New York, NY: PowerKids Press, 2012.

Stoker, Bram. *Dracula.* Adapted by Daniel Conner. Edina, MN: Magic Wagon, 2010.

Trumbauer, Lisa Trutkoff. *A Practical Guide to Vampires.* Renton, WA: Wizards of the Coast, 2009.

Websites

Bran Castle
www.bran-castle.com
Learn about the castle many consider to be the setting for Bram Stoker's *Dracula.*

The Real Dracula: Vlad the Impaler
www.livescience.com/40843-real-dracula-vlad-the-impaler.html
Read more about Vlad the Impaler.

Index

blood 4, 8, 9, 10, 12, 18, 22

Bran Castle 5

Dracula (book) 6, 8, 10, 11, 13, 16, 24, 28

Dracula (movie) 24, 28, 29

fangs 8

folklore 16, 18, 22, 24

garlic 16

Greek mythology 22

Lamia 22, 23

Lugosi, Bela 24, 25, 29

movies 4, 24, 26

nosferatu 8

Polidori, John 22

Romania 6, 8, 28

Sesame Street 27

stake 15, 18, 20

Stoker, Bram 6, 7, 8, 10, 11, 13, 16, 18, 24, 28

strigoi 16

Transylvania 5, 6, 14, 16, 17, 19, 26

Twilight 26

"Vampyre, The" 22

Van Helsing, Abraham 12, 14

Vlad Dracula 20, 21

Vlad the Impaler 18, 19, 20

Walachia 19, 20

Westenra, Lucy 12, 14